Old-Time Pickling and Spicing Recipes

Other books by Florence Brobeck

COOK IT IN A CASSEROLE

SERVE IT BUFFET

CHAFING DISH COOKERY

THE GOOD SALAD BOOK

COOKING WITH CURRY

Old-Time Pickling and Spicing Recipes

FLORENCE BROBECK

GRAMERCY PUBLISHING COMPANY · NEW YORK

This edition published by Gramercy Publishing Company,
a division of Crown Publishers, Inc.,
by arrangement with William Morrow & Co., Inc.

P

Contents

PICKLING AND SPICING TODAY

SMALLER HOUSEHOLDS, LIMITED PRESERVE shelves—or maybe not even one shelf for pickles and other good old-time homemade sweets and sours—that's the reason for this roundup of traditional recipes tested in small quantities. Pantry space, a cool cellar, a garden, an orchard, a farmer coming to the door with bushel baskets heaped with the harvest—these are not essential to winter enjoyment of good pickles, chutneys, preserves, and relishes at your table. In a kitchenette, small jars of your favorites can be prepared with ease. In the small kitchen of a busy young mother, business woman, or bachelor cook, the secret of success (shining filled jars), is to make only a small amount at a time when fruits and vegetables are at their best.

Buy a little at a time. Select fruit fully ripe and sound. Wash it carefully. Purchase only small amounts of fresh, young, perfect vegetables. Wash them through several waters. Visit Italian, Armenian, and other foreign markets and grocery stores for hot peppers, unusual spices, and other ingredients to make unusual mixtures.

Buy only a few glass jars, small ones. If you have old jars wash them in hot soapy water, rinse, then boil them 10 minutes in clear water with a tablespoon of soda added for every 2 quarts. Rinse well in boiling water. Boil old lids, if in good condition, 15 to 20 minutes and drain. Clean old lids can do no harm on pickled and spiced mixtures, but new jar rubbers are necessary no matter what goes in the jars. Have jars, caps, and rubbers newly scalded, standing by when the hot pickling mixture reaches the "done" point. This timing is easy after you once make a batch.

It's easier to use the kitchen scissors to cut fine, than to chop some ingredients. And use a paring knife to slice fruits and vegetables thin before chopping. Slice onions across, in round slices, never down from top to bottom; do the same with fruits and vegetables. In some mixtures appearance is half of it! Bread-and-butter pickles, for instance.

As for mincemeats, old-time cooks made quantities, cooked them, and sealed them for long-time storage. You will find it easy with these Ohio and Pennsylvania recipes to make your holiday mincemeat a few weeks before time to bake pies, tarts, and turnovers. Long cooking before canning is not necessary with these recipes; keep the mincemeat covered in the refrigerator or other cold place for a few weeks to ripen. Then use it up. Make more if you want some for January or late in the winter.

Make use of dried fruits any time of year. And for quick relishes, there are more than thirty recipes in this book. These combine bought pickles and ready-made dressings to make delicious condiments to garnish and enhance many dishes.

Label and date your filled jars so as to use brandied fruits when they are at their best, the spiced and pickled mixtures according to recipe timing. Keep jars on dark cool shelves, if possible, or in the coolest spot in the house.

Serve at least one pickled or spiced chutney, relish, butter, or sauce with every meal, for good flavor and appetite appeal. With buffet meals, offer a condiment tray containing four or more of your favorites. This will be the most patronized spot of the evening. Many of these modernized relishes are also perfect for barbecue meals; many are just right for make-it-yourself sandwich trays; all will make welcome gifts to family and friends.

New York   **Florence Brobeck**

WHAT YOU NEED FOR EFFICIENT SIMPLIFIED PICKLING

2 or more large (3- to 6-quart) agate or enamel kettles
Glass jars—quarts, pints, half-pints, jelly glasses, with tops, new
　　rubbers, sealers
Jar lifter
Thick pot holder
Dish towels
Tray for jars
1 or 2 large wooden spoons
1 or 2 large enamel spoons
Set measuring spoons
1 or 2 sharp paring knives
Measuring cups—1- and 2-cup sizes
Tea kettle for boiling water
Enamel colander
Sieve
Kitchen scissors
Wooden chopping bowl and chopper
Grater for lemon and orange peel
Food grinder
Juicer for lemons and oranges
Fresh whole and ground spices
High grade vinegars
Quality fruits, vegetables, herbs, and other ingredients
Gummed labels for filled jars
Paraffin

TO SEAL: If you buy new jars, follow directions which come
with them. In general, cover filled jars loosely with lid or cap;

let cool a little. Screw down cap and let cool further; tighten before storing. The rubber shrinks and it will not be tight enough after the first screwing of the lid or cap in place. Store in cool, airy, preferably dark place. See suggestions with recipes.

Old-Time Pickling and Spicing Recipes

usually other seasonings. The fruit, vegetables and season

1

Butters

THE TERM FRUIT OR VEGETABLE "BUTTER" does not hint at the deliciousness and adaptability of this old-time favorite. "A thick, smooth sauce," say the old cookbooks, "made by straining fruit or vegetables cooked with sugar and usually other seasonings." The fruit, vegetables and seasonings give distinctive color, texture, and the remembered flavor which make family and guests ask for such butters again and again.

Long, slow cooking—heat very low—is important to develop flavor, to blend the oils of the spices with the juices and sugars of the fruits, or with the tang and distinctive quality of the vegetables. Make small amounts at one time, and you will find it easier to serve if you bottle or seal in small jars. Then a jar, once opened, is quickly used up.

In Ohio, in my childhood, the year's supply of apple butter was always made as soon as my father brought the first cider home from the nearby cider mill. On a pleasant autumn day, in a great kettle hung on a tripod in the back yard, the butter cooked, a wood fire burning gently under it. To stir the butter, my father had made a long-handled paddle, perforated with smooth round holes. The fragrant hot butter streamed through and around the big paddle as it moved back and forth through the cooking mixture. The whole neighborhood sprawled under the trees and on our back porch or hung over the fence, not only to help with the fire and the stirring, and to enjoy the good smell which filled the air, but to carry home a jar of the delicious dark butter at the end of the day.

Sunday night supper at home, the whole winter through, featured a bowl of apple butter to be eaten with freshly made schmierkäse (homemade cottage cheese) on fresh-baked bread or biscuits. It was wonderful!

APPLE BUTTER

one of the best old-time spreads.

3 quarts fresh sweet cider
8 pounds juicy ripe apples, washed, cored, and quartered
2½ cups (packed) brown sugar
2 teaspoons powdered cinnamon
½ teaspoon powdered allspice
½ teaspoon powdered cloves
½ teaspoon salt

Boil cider in large agate or enamel kettle until amount is reduced one-half, about 30 minutes. Add apples and cook over low heat until tender. Stir almost constantly with wooden spoon or paddle. When apples are completely cooked, force mixture through sieve. Return to kettle; add sugar, spices, and salt; cook over low heat, stirring until sugar is dissolved. Then cook until mixture thickens, about 30 minutes. (Use asbestos mat under kettle to insure low heat, if necessary.) Stir almost continually. Pour at once into hot sterile jars and seal at once. Makes 4 pints.

NOTE: For apple butter you can use Jonathan, McIntosh, Russet, or Winesap apples.

CALIFORNIA APPLE BUTTER

light in color, mild in flavor, a delicious spread.

2 cups dried apples
2½ cups water
1 cup sugar
½ teaspoon powdered cinnamon
¼ teaspoon powdered allspice

Rinse apples, drain, add water, and cook, covered, 20 to 30 minutes, or until apples are tender. Force through sieve to remove any bits of skin or core. Add sugar and spices to pulp. Cover and cook slowly, 20 to 30 minutes longer, or until desired consistency. Seal at once in sterile glass jars. Makes 1 to 1½ pints.

CONCORD GRAPE BUTTER

a fine flavor with game, curries, turkey sandwiches.

2 pounds Concord grapes
1½ tablespoons grated orange peel
1 cup water
2¼ cups sugar
½ teaspoon powdered cinnamon
¼ teaspoon powdered cloves
⅛ teaspoon grated nutmeg

Wash grapes, drain, and pull from stems. Squeeze pulp from skins into agate or enamel kettle. Cook pulp slowly until soft, about 10 minutes. Put through sieve to remove seeds. Return pulp to kettle; add orange peel and water; cook 10 minutes, stirring frequently with wooden or enamel spoon. Add skins; heat to boiling; add sugar and spices; stir; cook over low heat until thick. Stir frequently. Seal at once in hot sterile glasses. Makes 6 or 7 six-ounce glasses.

DRIED FRUITS BUTTER

can be made at any season, and used at once.

3 cups prunes
3 cups dried apricots
¾ cup sugar
¼ teaspoon salt
¼ teaspoon powdered cinnamon
¼ teaspoon powdered cloves
¾ cup combined prune and apricot liquids

Rinse prunes, cover with cold water and boil slowly 45 minutes to 1 hour. Rinse apricots, cover with cold water and boil 30 to 40 minutes. Drain fruits and save liquids. Remove prune pits. Force fruits through colander or sieve. Combine purées, sugar, salt, spice and ¾ cup liquids. Return to heat and boil briskly 12 to 15 minutes, stirring continually to prevent scorching. If purées are very dry, a little more liquid may be added before cooking down. Seal in sterile glasses or jar. Makes 1 pint butter.

GINGERED TOMATO BUTTER

good with almost anything—especially fish and sausage.

1½ pounds red tomatoes
3½ pounds green tomatoes, washed and chopped
2 lemons
2½ cups sugar
½ teaspoon powdered cloves
2 small pieces ginger root
1 tablespoon finely-chopped candied or preserved ginger
1 tablespoon finely-chopped candied orange peel

Scald, peel, and quarter red tomatoes; combine with green tomatoes in agate or enamel kettle. Wash lemons; slice very thin; remove seeds. Add to tomatoes with sugar, seasonings, ginger, and orange peel. Cook over low heat, stirring frequently with wooden or enamel spoon until thick, about 30 minutes. (Time varies with juiciness of tomatoes.) Seal in hot sterile glass jars. Makes about 3 pints.

RED PEPPER BUTTER

for a cold morning with hot grilled sausages and biscuits!

15 sweet red peppers
2 cups chopped peeled dead-ripe tomatoes, or 2 cups canned
  tomatoes
1 cup water
Lemons
Oranges
Seedless raisins
½ cup drained maraschino cherries
Citron
Sugar
Salt

Wash peppers, drain, cut in half, and remove seeds and fibers. Put peppers through food grinder, using fine knife. Place ground peppers in agate or enamel kettle with water and tomatoes. Cook slowly until peppers are mushy, stirring constantly. Pass through sieve. Measure and return to kettle. For 4 cups of pepper mixture, add: juice 1 lemon, juice 1 orange, 1 cup seedless raisins, which have been soaked and drained, ½ cup chopped maraschino cherries, 1 tablespoon finely-cut citron, 1⅓ cups sugar, and 1 teaspoon salt. Mix. Cook slowly until mixture is very thick. Stir almost constantly, but slowly, with wooden or enamel spoon. Pour into hot sterile glasses or jars. Cover with paraffin; store in cool place. Makes 3 eight-ounce jelly glasses.

SPICED CONCORD GRAPE BUTTER

takes time, but the results are worth it.

3 pounds Concord grapes
1/2 cup cider vinegar
3 cups sugar
1 1/2 teaspoons powdered cinnamon
3/4 teaspoon powdered cloves
1/4 teaspoon salt

Wash grapes; drain; press out of skins, saving skins and pulp. Cook pulp, covered, in agate or enamel kettle until soft, about 10 minutes. Stir frequently with wooden or enamel spoon. Rub cooked pulp through sieve to remove seeds. Heat vinegar, sugar, spices, and salt together in kettle; add skins and sieved pulp. Cook over low heat, boiling gently about 20 minutes, and stirring constantly though slowly. When juice thickens to jamlike consistency, pour into hot sterile glass jars; seal at once. Makes 2 pints.

SPICED PRUNE BUTTER I

can be made any time. Good eating summer and winter.

1 pound prunes
1 cup sugar
1/2 cup white or cider vinegar
1/2 teaspoon powdered cinnamon
1/4 teaspoon grated nutmeg
1/2 teaspoon powdered allspice
1/4 teaspoon powdered cloves
1/8 teaspoon pepper

Rinse prunes, cover with water, bring to boiling, and boil slowly 40 to 45 minutes, or until tender. Cool, drain, cut from pits in halves or quarters. Add remaining ingredients and boil 5 minutes. Seal in hot sterile glass jars or 8-ounce jelly glasses. Makes 1½ pints.

SPICED PRUNE BUTTER II

a spread for Boston brown bread or hot buttered cornbread.

1 pound prunes, washed, soaked overnight
1 quart water
1 large orange
1/2 cup seedless raisins, soaked and drained
3 cups sugar
1/2 teaspoon powdered cloves
1/2 teaspoon powdered cinnamon
1/4 teaspoon powdered ginger
1/2 cup chopped pecans or walnuts

Drain prunes; remove pits. Combine prunes and water in agate or enamel kettle. Cut peel from orange, chop or cut thin with scissors; add to prunes. Slice orange very thin; cut slices in half; remove seeds; add slices to prunes. Bring to boiling and boil 10 minutes. Add raisins, sugar, and spices. Stir over low heat until sugar dissolves. Continue to cook and stir until thickened, about 10 minutes. Stir in nuts. Pour into hot sterile glass jars and seal. Makes 2½ pints.

2

Catsups

THE BRIGHT, GLOWING COLOR OF COMMERCIAL catsup results from methods and formulae which only large-scale cannery-cooking and processing can achieve. "Color isn't everything," might be the slogan of the home catsup-maker. The fine flavor, and variety, which she can stir into the catsup kettle result in delicious condiments for sandwiches, cold meats, and many other table delicacies.

Catsup is a finely-chopped, sieved fruit or vegetable, cooked and strained to make a smooth, thick sauce. It should be highly spiced, while retaining the distinctive flavor of the fruit or vegetables in it. Its purpose in early English homes was to *disguise* the flavor of meats—an unavoidable necessity which refrigeration has remedied.

CALIFORNIA PEACH CATSUP

make and keep in refrigerator to serve cold at any time.

1 No. 2½ can cling peach slices
1 large onion, washed, peeled, and chopped
½ cup white or cider vinegar
½ teaspoon powdered cloves
½ teaspoon powdered cinnamon
¼ teaspoon powdered allspice
¼ teaspoon salt
Dash Tabasco sauce

Drain sirup from peaches; boil down in agate or enamel kettle to about ½ cup. Add peaches, onion, and remaining ingredients. Cover; boil slowly until onion and peaches are soft and mixture is thick, about 1 hour. Stir frequently with wooden or enamel spoon. Let cool slightly and put through sieve. Pour into 1-pint sterile glass jar, and store in refrigerator. Makes about 1¾ cups.

CUCUMBER CATSUP

add to salad dressing or serve with cold cuts.

6 large (6-inch) cucumbers
1 medium-sized onion, peeled and grated
¾ teaspoon freshly-ground pepper
1 teaspoon salt
1 cup cider vinegar (about)

Wash cucumbers, drain, cover with cold water, and let stand 1 to 2 hours. Drain, pare, grate or grind as fine as possible into bowl or glass jar. Add remaining ingredients with just enough vinegar to make a smooth consistency. Mash, mix well, and press through sieve. Keep in covered quart jar in refrigerator. Makes about 2 pints.

GRAPE CATSUP

another old-time favorite with hot or cold game and meats.

5 pints grapes, washed and pulled from stems
4 cups (packed) brown sugar
I pint cider vinegar
2 tablespoons powdered allspice
2 tablespoons powdered cinnamon
2 tablespoons powdered cloves
I teaspoon powdered mace
¾ teaspoon cayenne
I teaspoon salt

Cook grapes in agate or enamel kettle slowly, until soft, about 25 minutes. Put through colander. Combine with remaining ingredients; boil until thick, about 45 minutes. Stir frequently with enamel spoon. Pour into hot sterile glass jar. Makes 1 pint.

TOMATO CATSUP

a tasty, delicious catsup, darker than bought catsup.

4½ pounds ripe red tomatoes
Boiling water
1 sweet red pepper
2 medium-sized onions, peeled and quartered
½ teaspoon whole allspice
½ teaspoon whole cloves
2 (three-inch) sticks cinnamon, broken
½ teaspoon celery seeds
½ teaspoon dry mustard
1 teaspoon paprika and ¼ teaspoon cayenne
1 teaspoon salt and ½ cup sugar
½ cup cider vinegar

Wash tomatoes, pour boiling water over, and let stand 5 minutes. Rub off loosened skins, cut out stem ends, and quarter. Wash pepper, drain, and cut in half. Remove seeds and fibers and cut into thin strips. Put all vegetables through grinder together, using fine knife. Cook in agate or enamel kettle over low heat about 30 minutes; stir frequently with wooden or enamel spoon. Press cooked vegetables through fine agate or enamel colander; return to kettle; bring to boiling, and boil 30 minutes, until mixture is slightly thickened. Stir frequently. Tie up allspice, cloves, and cinnamon in small piece of cheese-cloth; add to kettle with remaining spices, sugar, and vinegar. Stir until sugar is dissolved; continue cooking over low heat until very thick, about like commercial catsup. Stir frequently. Remove spice bag. Pour hot catsup into hot sterile glass jars; seal at once. Makes about 2 pints.

TOMATO GARLIC CATSUP

a fine barbecue catsup; men like this one.

4 No. 2 cans tomatoes, or
   4 pounds ripe tomatoes
2 tablespoons salt
I cup sugar
½ teaspoon cayenne
2 tablespoons powdered ginger
6 garlic cloves, chopped
¼ teaspoon dry mustard

Combine all ingredients in agate or enamel kettle. Boil slowly, stirring frequently with enamel spoon, until mixture is reduced to about half, about 1 hour or longer. Strain through sieve; reheat just to boiling. Seal at once in hot sterile glass jars. Makes about 3 pints.

NOTE: For most tastes, the amount of garlic should be reduced to 1 or 2 buds. Also, if garlic and spices are tied in a cheese-cloth bag, and removed before catsup is strained, the color of the finished catsup will be better.

VARIATION: Omit garlic; add 3 medium-sized green peppers, seeds and fibers removed, and 3 medium-sized onions, peeled, all chopped very fine. Then cook.

3

Chutneys

CHUTNEY IS ORIENTAL IN ORIGIN. THE VARIETY
of fruits, spices, and flavorsome vegetables, nuts, and berries,
which abound in the Orient, inspired the spicy mixture
known as chutney. Its purpose, like that of catsup, was to *disguise* the flavor of game, meat, fowl, and other foods. More
recently, by choice, for its fine flavor, it appears on menus
as condiment and accessory—not as an essential.

The most familiar use of chutney in the Orient is with
curries. British civil servants and army officials stationed
in India brought back chutneys to London, and by the

eighteenth century, London picklers were making several varieties.

Chutney is defined as a highly-seasoned sweet pickle, relish, or catsup. In some parts of America it is nothing more than a pickle relish. In others, a chutney resembles the Indian type with ginger, raisins, and sweetly-spiced sirups. So take your choice. If you want to call your pet relish a chutney, there is no one to stop you. If you want to garnish your favorite curried dishes à la India, however, the chutney will be sweet and spicy.

APPLE AND PEPPER CHUTNEY

delicious! fine with game, ham, curries, any hot roast.

2 cups (packed) brown sugar

1 quart white vinegar

2 tablespoons mustard seeds

2 tablespoons salt

2 teaspoons ground coriander seeds

2 teaspoons powdered cloves

6 green tomatoes, washed and chopped fine

4 small onions, washed, peeled, chopped fine

2 green peppers, washed, chopped fine, seeds and fibers removed

1 cup seedless raisins, soaked and drained

1 cup dried currants, soaked and drained

12 medium-sized eating apples, washed, peeled, cored, chopped coarsely

1 cup water

Dissolve sugar in vinegar in an agate or enamel kettle; add mustard seeds, salt, coriander, and cloves. Bring to boiling. Add tomatoes, onions, peppers, raisins, and currants. Let simmer 40 minutes; stir frequently with wooden or enamel spoon. Add apples and water, mix, bring to boiling, and cover. Cook gently about 30 minutes, or until apples are soft. Stir from time to time with wooden or enamel spoon. Seal in sterile glass jars. Makes 5 pints.

CALIFORNIA CHUTNEY

a fine condiment with curried shrimps or chicken.

1 cup prunes
1 cup seedless raisins
1½ cups pear or cider vinegar
2 cups (packed) brown sugar
1 teaspoon dry mustard
½ teaspoon powdered cinnamon
½ teaspoon salt
⅛ teaspoon cayenne
2 cups chopped, washed, peeled, and cored apples
1 cup washed, chopped, peeled onions
1 cup peeled, chopped, fresh or canned tomatoes

Cover prunes with water and boil 10 minutes. Drain; cut fruit from pits into small pieces. Rinse and drain raisins. Combine vinegar, sugar, mustard, cinnamon, salt, and cayenne in agate or enamel kettle. Heat to boiling; add apples, prunes, raisins, onions, and tomatoes. Boil, covered, stirring frequently with wooden or enamel spoon. When mixture is desired consistency, in about 30 minutes, pour into hot sterile glass jars and seal at once. Makes 2 pints.

PEACH CHUTNEY

wonderful with barbecued meats and many other dishes.

2 No. 2½ cans cling peach slices
1 green pepper, seeds and fibers removed
1 large onion, washed and peeled
½ cup seedless raisins
1 cup (packed) brown sugar
1½ cups white or cider vinegar
¼ cup chopped preserved ginger
½ teaspoon salt
¼ teaspoon powdered cloves
¼ teaspoon grated nutmeg
¼ to ½ teaspoon cayenne
¼ teaspoon black pepper

Drain peaches. (Use up sirup in sauces and fruit salad dressings.) Chop pepper and onion; rinse and drain raisins; Combine all ingredients in agate or enamel kettle, cover, simmer 1 to 1½ hours, or until thick. Uncover to let cook down if necessary. Seal hot in sterile glass jars. Makes 2 pints.

Brandied Fruits

THE FLAVORING OF FRUITS WITH A FINE BRANDY
or wine goes back to early Rome and Greece when Lucullan
feasts called for wine in almost everything served. To dip berries and fruits into a cup of wine added just that much
more pleasure to the banquet. Fruit and wine or fruit and
brandy are happy affinities. The flavor of a long-brandied
fruit is especially harmonious with the delicacy of superbly-
cooked chicken or a fine sugared ham or as the fruity-
farewell of a rather bland dinner which, until the brandied
dessert, lacked that essential, distinctive appetite satisfaction.

The hearty appetites of eighteenth-century Englishmen

(who lived in style) and their relatives in Virginia and other locations in the New World encouraged housewives to put down fruits in fine brandy. The custom spread westward with the settlement of the country until brandied fruits became familiar on the pantry shelves and in the cellar cold rooms everywhere.

BRANDIED CHERRIES

delicious *flambé* on vanilla ice cream or pound cake.

1 cup cooked or canned dark oxheart cherries
Cognac
2 tablespoons kirsch or cointreau
2 tablespoons sugar
1/2 teaspoon powdered cinnamon
1/4 teaspoon powdered cloves

Combine cherries, about 1/4 cup cognac, and remaining ingredients in a pint glass jar; keep covered in refrigerator until ready to serve. Then turn mixture into chafing dish and heat. Pour more cognac into a tablespoon; light it with a match; pour over cherries; stir. When flame dies down, spoon hot cherries over dessert. Makes 4 servings.

NOTE: This mixture can be made in quantity, sealed in a sterile jar, and kept for ready use. Add about 1 tablespoon cognac to flame 1 cup cherries. If cherry preserves are used, omit sugar and spices.

EASY BRANDIED PEACHES

serve as desert or as part of fruit salad or compote.

2 pounds small ripe peaches
1½ pounds sugar
1 cup water
Cognac

Wash, scald and peel peaches; leave whole. Boil sugar
and water together 5 minutes in agate or enamel kettle. Add
peaches a few at a time; boil until fruit is tender, about 15
minutes. Spoon peaches into a hot, sterile, glass jar, quart-size.
Let the sirup boil down a little, but do not scrape sides of pan
or sirup will be sugary. Add hot sirup alternately with equal
amount of cognac to fill the jar. Seal at once. Store in dark
cool place for 3 to 4 months. Makes 1 quart.

COUNTRY BRANDIED PEACHES

makes a darker peach of excellent flavor.

2 pounds perfect, ripe peaches
Boiling water
1½ pounds sugar
Cognac

Wash peaches; scald in boiling water about 5 minutes; pull off loosened skin. Place peaches and sugar in layers in a stone crock or jar. To each quart of peaches add ½ cup cognac. Cover with cheesecloth, then with lid of crock or jar. Let stand in cool, dark place 6 weeks; remove scum; seal peaches and brandied juice in hot sterile jar. Let stand another month before serving. Makes 1 quart.

5

Mincemeats

MEAT WAS SCARCE IN EIGHTEENTH-CENTURY
English homes; every scrap must have been a challenge to the
ingenuity of the cooks in those cumbersome, dark, and dreary
kitchens. To mince up the remains of the roast, to mix with it
a little fruit, or some vegetables, to add the always-essential
spice (as a preservative), and then to bake it all in a pie—
almost as good as a *real* beef or pork pie—might well have
been the origin of the mixture long ago named mincemeat.
It makes the heartiest of all pies; it is eaten hot or cold.
It should have a bit of brandy, wine, whisky, or, lacking
these, fruit juice added before baking.

Old American cookbooks abound in mincemeat recipes, some dark and of strangely dull taste; others too spicy or too heavy. Here are three unusual recipes of fresh flavor and appeal. You can store these mincemeats upside down for a few days. Then turn the jars right side up so the mixture of molasses-liquid distributes itself evenly. Before filling tart shells or a pastry-lined pie plate, sprinkle mincemeat with 2 to 3 tablespoons of cognac, whisky, sherry or port wine, grape or orange juice. Mix and use at once.

CHRISTMAS MINCEMEAT

1/2 cup finely-chopped suet
1/2 cup washed, scraped, and grated carrots
6 large eating apples, washed, peeled, cored, and chopped
2 cups seeded raisins, or currants, soaked and drained
1/2 cup ground leftover cooked beef, or cooked hamburger
1/2 cup finely-cut citron
1/2 cup finely-cut candied orange peel
2 tablespoons powdered cinnamon
1/2 tablespoon grated nutmeg
1/2 tablespoon powdered cloves
1 1/2 cups light molasses, or
    1 cup brown sugar, and
    1/2 cup water
2 cups boiled cider

Mix all together in agate or enamel kettle; bring to boiling, and boil 5 minutes. Pack at once into hot sterile glass jars and seal. Set in cool place 10 days to ripen. Makes 6 pints.

GREEN TOMATO MINCEMEAT

1 quart chopped washed green tomatoes
2 tablespoons salt
1 cup light corn sirup
1½ cups sweet cider
1 cup boiled sweet cider
¾ cup finely-chopped suet
5 eating apples, washed, peeled, cored, and chopped
1 carrot, washed, scraped, and grated
2 cups seedless raisins, soaked and drained
2 cups (two 7¼-ounce packages) seedless dried dates
1 cup (7-ounce package) cut dried figs, stems removed
½ cup chopped salted or plain peanuts or almonds
1½ tablespoons powdered cinnamon
1 tablespoon powdered cloves
½ tablespoon grated nutmeg
½ tablespoon powdered ginger
1½ cups light molasses

Put tomatoes in a colander, sprinkle with salt, and let drain 1 hour. Place in an agate or enamel kettle with sirup and the 1½ cups sweet cider. Cover and cook gently 15 minutes; stir with wooden or enamel spoon. Stir in remaining ingredients. Cook 10 minutes more, stirring frequently. Seal in hot sterile glass jars. Makes 4 pints.

OHIO FRUIT MINCEMEAT

3 large oranges, grated peel and juice only
6 eating apples, washed, peeled, cored, and chopped
1 cup chopped suet
1 cup seedless raisins, soaked and drained
1 cup finely-cut dried peaches, soaked and drained
1 cup finely-cut dried apricots, soaked and drained
1/2 cup finely-cut citron
1 cup grated or ground scraped, washed carrots
2 tablespoons powdered cinnamon
1/2 tablespoon powdered allspice
1/2 teaspoon powdered mace
1/2 tablespoon powdered ginger
1 teaspoon powdered cloves
2 cups light molasses
3/4 cup (packed) brown sugar
1 cup boiled cider

Mix all ingredients in an agate or enamel kettle, or large bowl. Pour into sterile glass jars. Seal. Store in refrigerator or dark, cool place to ripen at least 10 days before using. Unusually good. Makes 6 pints.

6

Pickles of All Kinds

TO MOST PEOPLE, PICKLES MEAN CUCUMBERS preserved in a salty or sweet vinegar mixture. But the term has a much broader use in cookery, where combinations of cucumbers, onions, other vegetables, and fruits, variously assorted, in flavored vinegars are called pickles.

These sour, spicy foods have always been favorites on American tables. The fact that so many good ones are available at the grocery store need not keep a homemaker from putting up a few jars of pickles every summer. Homemade pickles have a quality difficult to duplicate by the big canners. Hence the popularity of small-kitchen canners, "home" picklers, who sell their favorites through speciality grocers, by mail order, and in gift shops.

These recipes are selected from many parts of the country where good cookery is legend. Some of them are Southern recipes; several are New England, and the Pennsylvania Dutch and Ohio pickles are here too.

AUNT JENNY'S CROCK PICKLES

a spicy sweet pickle, good with sandwiches and cold cuts.

2 quarts cider vinegar
1 medium-sized onion, washed, peeled, and sliced
2 tablespoons dry mustard
2 tablespoons salt
1/2 ounce white ginger root
2 tablespoons whole cloves
2 (three-inch) sticks cinnamon, broken
1 tablespoon whole peppercorns
1 tablespoon powdered cloves
1/2 pound (1⅜ cups packed) brown sugar
2 quarts midget cucumbers, washed and drained

Mix all ingredients, except cucumbers, together in a 1-gallon crock, or large glass jar. Add cucumbers. Cover crock or jar with folded cheesecloth, then with lid. Let stand in cool dark place at least 1 month before using. Better if allowed to stand 3 months. Makes 2 quarts pickles.

EAST INDIA CURRIED PICKLES

misleading title, actually a sour cucumber pickle spiced with curry.

6 large cucumbers, washed, pared, and sliced
6 medium-sized onions, washed, peeled, and sliced
Salt
1 quart white or wine vinegar
1½ cups (packed) brown sugar
1 small hot red pepper
1 tablespoon curry powder
1 teaspoon celery seeds
1 teaspoon mustard seeds
½ teaspoon freshly-ground black pepper
Small bag (2 tablespoons) mixed whole pickling spices

Combine cucumbers and onions in large bowl; sprinkle salt (about ½ cup) generously over layers. Add water barely to cover. Let stand in cool place overnight. Drain; wash vegetables under running cold water. Drain thoroughly. Spoon into sterile glass jars. Combine remaining ingredients in agate or enamel kettle; cover and boil gently about 10 minutes. Remove spice bag. Pour hot vinegar mixture over cucumbers and onions in jars. Seal at once. Let stand a few weeks in cool dark place before using. Makes 3 pints.

NOTE: This is good served as a first course with herring, or pâté, or with a hot cheese canapé.

ENGLISH CHOWCHOW

hot, sour, delicious. Serve with meat loaf, curries, boiled beef tongue.

8 medium-sized (3- to 4-inch) cucumbers
I quart string beans, washed, tips and strings removed
I quart chopped washed green tomatoes
I medium-sized head cauliflower, washed and broken into
   flowerets
I small head cabbage, washed and chopped fine
I quart small white onions, washed and peeled
Salt
⅓ cup dry mustard
I teaspoon turmeric
3 hot red peppers, very small fresh or dried type, washed
   and stemmed
2 tablespoons mustard seeds
I tablespoon celery seeds
I tablespoon whole allspice
I tablespoon whole cloves
½ cup sugar
Cider vinegar

Put all vegetables through food grinder using medium-coarse knife. Mix thoroughly in large agate or enamel kettle. Sprinkle lightly with salt (about ½ cup); cover; let stand in cool place 24 hours. Drain brine off. Heat vegetables over low heat; stir in all seasonings and mix well. Pour over vinegar (about 4 cups) barely to cover. Cover kettle; let simmer, stirring often with wooden or enamel spoon. When vegetables are cooked, about ½ hour, spoon into hot sterile glass jars and seal. Makes 6 pints.

HOMEMADE CAPERS

add to sauce for fish or to salad mixtures.

2 cups fresh green nasturtium seeds
1 cup water
¼ cup salt
1 cup sugar
1 cup cider vinegar

Wash and drain seeds. Mix water and salt; pour over seeds in jar or crock. Cover and let stand 2 days. Drain seeds and pour into sterile glass jar. Heat sugar and vinegar to boiling; pour over seeds. Seal. Makes 1 pint.

NOTE: Only country housewives with a row of nasturtiums along the garden fence can make this easy pickle. The sour little capers are so good added to salads, to bland sauces for boiled meat or fish, or used as a tart garnish around an aspic.

LUCINDA'S BREAD-AND-BUTTER PICKLES

an old Ohio recipe of superb flavor. Keep some covered in refrigerator.

4 pounds (10 to 12 small) cucumbers, washed, pared, and cubed
4 medium-sized onions, washed, peeled, and sliced
$\frac{1}{4}$ cup salt
$1\frac{1}{2}$ cups (packed) brown sugar
1 pint cider vinegar
2 (three-inch) sticks cinnamon, broken
1 teaspoon whole allspice
1 teaspoon white mustard seeds
$\frac{1}{2}$ teaspoon turmeric
$\frac{1}{2}$ teaspoon celery seeds
$\frac{1}{8}$ teaspoon cayenne

Place cucumbers and onions in layers in separate glass or earthenware bowls, each layer sprinkled generously with salt. Cover and let stand overnight. In the morning, drain vegetables, rinse well with cold water and drain thoroughly. Combine cucumbers and onions. Dissolve sugar in vinegar in a 3-quart agate or enamel kettle. Tie cinnamon and allspice together in a small cheesecloth bag. Add to hot vinegar. Boil 1 to 2 minutes. Stir in remaining ingredients. Add drained cucumbers and onions; let scald thoroughly in hot vinegar, 25 to 30 minutes, over very low heat, but do not boil. Remove spice bag. Spoon pickle into hot sterile glass jars; seal at once. Let stand a few weeks before using. Makes 2 pints.

PENNSYLVANIA DUTCH MUSTARD PICKLES

any leftover sirup is a flavorful addition to salad dressing.

1 quart (about 2 pounds) sliced, washed green tomatoes
1 quart (about 2 pounds) small onions, washed, peeled, and sliced
1 quart (about 2 pounds) sliced, washed string beans, tips removed
1 large head cauliflower, washed, broken in flowerets
10 medium-sized cucumbers, washed, pared, sliced
¾ cup salt
½ pound dry mustard
4 tablespoons cornstarch or flour
1 cup water
1 teaspoon turmeric
1½ quarts cider vinegar
3 cups sugar

Combine all vegetables in a large agate or enamel kettle, in layers sprinkled with salt. Cover; let stand in a cool place overnight. In the morning, drain thoroughly. Mix mustard, cornstarch or flour, water, and turmeric; combine with vinegar and sugar in another agate or enamel kettle; heat to boiling, stirring frequently. Pour over vegetables; heat slowly to boiling; boil gently 15 minutes. Pull kettle aside and let stand a few minutes. Stir, reheat to boiling, and boil 15 minutes. Spoon into hot sterile glass jars; seal at once. Makes about 6 pints.

PENNSYLVANIA DUTCH SALT PICKLES

good with beer and cheese, bread and butter,
and Saturday night ham.

2 quarts midget cucumbers
Salt
2 or 3 sprays fresh dill
2 tablespoons mixed fresh or dried herbs (oregano, thyme, marjoram mint, basil)
I tablespoon mustard seeds
I tablespoon powdered ginger
10 whole cloves
10 whole peppercorns
3 cups water
3 cups cider vinegar
¾ cup salt

Wash and drain cucumbers. Place in 3-quart or 1-gallon stone jar or large glass jar. Cover top with layer of salt ⅜-inch thick. Pour fresh cold water over to cover well; place weight on cucumbers; let stand in cool place 3 weeks. At that time, drain the pickles, wash under running cold water. Return to jar arranging in layers with dill, herbs, mustard seeds, ginger, cloves, and peppercorns. Boil water, vinegar, and ¾ cup salt together 3 minutes in an agate or enamel kettle; pour warm over the drained pickles. The liquid should cover them by 2 inches. Cover and place weight on the lid; let stand at least 1 month before using. Makes 2 quarts pickles.

PICCALILLI

so good with hot or cold baked beans or on sandwich tray.

4 pounds green tomatoes, washed and drained
6 medium-sized onions, washed, peeled, and sliced
1/2 cup salt
2 small green peppers, washed, seeds and fibers removed, chopped
2 cups sugar
I pint cider vinegar
2 tablespoons celery seeds
2 tablespoons mustard seeds
I tablespoon whole cloves
I teaspoon peppercorns
2 (two-inch) sticks cinnamon, broken

Slice tomatoes very thin. Place layers of tomatoes and onions, sprinkled with salt, in large bowl. Cover and let stand in cool place overnight. Drain and rinse well with cold water. Drain and pour into agate or enamel kettle. Add peppers to kettle, with sugar, vinegar, celery and mustard seeds. Tie remaining spices in small cheesecloth bag; add to kettle. Stir with wooden or enamel spoon until sugar dissolves. Bring to boiling, and boil rapidly 15 minutes. Remove spice bag. Spoon pickle into hot sterile glass jars and seal. Let stand several weeks before using. Makes about 3 pints.

PICKAWAY COUNTY GREEN TOMATO PICKLE

one of the Seven Sours of the old Pennsylvania Dutch families.

½ peck (about 8 pounds) green tomatoes, washed and chopped
⅓ cup salt
¼ cup grated fresh or prepared horse-radish
½ tablespoon powdered cinnamon
½ tablespoon powdered cloves
½ tablespoon powdered allspice
½ tablespoon dry mustard
1 tablespoon freshly-ground pepper
1 cup (packed) brown sugar
Cider vinegar

Place tomatoes in an agate or enamel kettle; sprinkle with salt. Cover, and let stand in cool place overnight. Next morning let mixture drain in colander. Rinse quickly and drain again. Return tomatoes to kettle; mix remaining ingredients with 2 cups vinegar and pour over the tomatoes; then add enough vinegar to cover. Bring to boiling, cover, boil slowly 20 minutes. Stir a few times with enamel or wooden spoon only to distribute spice. Pour into sterile glass jars; seal at once. Let stand a month or longer before using. Makes 4 pints.

PICKLED ONIONS

serve with curry or with hot boiled beef and horse-radish sauce.

3 quarts small white onions, scalded, drained and peeled
1/2 cup salt
1 quart water
1 small chili pepper
1/2 teaspoon peppercorns
4 (one-inch) pieces ginger root
1 cup sugar (about)
3 pints white vinegar

Drain onions, cover with cold water, and drain again. Dissolve salt in 1 quart water in an agate or enamel kettle; add onions and enough water to cover. Let stand overnight, rinse in cold water, and drain. Heat enough water to cover onions; when boiling add onions and boil 1 minute. Drain. Spoon into hot, sterile glass jars, arranging in layers with a bit of finely-cut chili pepper, peppercorns, and ginger root. Heat sugar and vinegar together in agate or enamel kettle; when boiling pour over onions to within half an inch of top of jar. Adjust lids; place jars on a rack in a kettle half full of boiling water and boil water 15 minutes. Remove jars; complete seal. Makes about 4 pints.

NOTE: Place wooden rack in bottom of kettle of boiling water. Lift hot jars with jar holder.

SLICED OLIVE-OIL PICKLES

Italian cooks use chopped fennel in place of mixed herbs.

12 (three-inch) cucumbers washed, sliced thin
1 medium-sized onion, washed, peeled, and sliced thin
1/4 cup coarse salt
1 cup cider vinegar
1 cup water
1 1/4 teaspoons powdered alum
2 tablespoons white mustard seeds
1 tablespoon black mustard seeds
3/4 teaspoon celery seeds
2 teaspoons mixed dried herbs (oregano, basil, parsley)
1/2 cup olive oil (about)

Cucumbers should measure about 2 1/2 quarts. Arrange in layers with onion and salt in crock or bowl. Let stand overnight. Drain; place onion in one bowl and cucumbers in another. Combine vinegar and water; dissolve alum in half the vinegar mixture. Pour over cucumbers; let stand covered 4 to 5 hours. Drain; combine cucumbers with onion again and add mixed seasonings. Pack into sterile glass jars. Mix olive oil with remaining half of vinegar-and-water mixture. Do not heat; pour at once over pickles; seal. Let stand at least 4 weeks before using. Makes 4 pints.

NOTE: Vinegar-and-water mixture may have to be increased, depending on size of cucumbers and onion; if so, add proportionate extra amount of olive oil.

STUFFED PICKLED PEPPERS

a lot of trouble but a conversation piece when finished.

Old-time cooks called these and stuffed whole fruits "mangoes."
They were favorites in English-American homes because the flavor
is superb with baked ham, game, roast pork, and with baked beans.
Serve whole as a salad, or slice and use as garnish.

12 medium-sized green peppers
2 cups finely-chopped cabbage
1 cup chopped peeled onions
1/2 cup chopped green peppers
1/2 cup chopped sweet red peppers
1/2 cup chopped celery
1 tablespoon mustard seeds
1/2 tablespoon celery seeds
1/4 cup grated fresh or prepared horse-radish
1/4 cup salt
1/4 cup (packed) brown sugar
1 pint cider vinegar
1/2 teaspoon cayenne
1 teaspoon paprika
1/2 teaspoon dry mustard

Wash all vegetables thoroughly before chopping; drain
peppers; cut off tops and save; remove seeds and membranes.
Cover tops and peppers with water and bring to boiling; boil
gently 10 minutes, or until almost tender. Drain, and let cool.
Combine chopped vegetables. Mix remaining ingredients; pour
over vegetables and mix well. Stuff into peppers; do not pack
too tightly. Place top on each pepper. Tie in place with string.

Place peppers in wide-mouthed jars or in a large crock or jar. Heat together in agate or enamel kettle all of the following ingredients *except olive oil*:

3 pints cider vinegar
I quart water
½ cup salt
I tablespoon celery seeds
1½ tablespoons mustard seeds
4 tablespoons whole cloves
2 tablespoons whole allspice
I (three-inch) stick cinnamon, broken
2 blades mace, or
I teaspoon ground mace
Olive oil

Bring spice mixture to boiling; pour over stuffed peppers. Let cool. To each 3 peppers in jar or crock add about ½ cup olive oil. Cover. Let stand in cool place 10 days or longer before using. To serve, remove string, drain stuffed peppers and serve whole as garnish or salad. Makes 12 stuffed peppers.

NOTE: Use remaining oil and spice mixture in salad dressings or for marinade.

SWEET CUCUMBER PICKLES

for these delicious pickles use gherkins or slightly larger cucumbers.

25 small cucumbers
1 quart boiling water
$\frac{1}{2}$ cup salt
$1\frac{1}{2}$ quarts cider or white vinegar
1 pint water
$\frac{1}{2}$ tablespoon whole allspice
$\frac{1}{2}$ tablespoon peppercorns
$\frac{1}{2}$ tablespoon whole cloves
$\frac{1}{2}$ tablespoon celery seeds
$\frac{1}{2}$ tablespoon mustard seeds
1 (two-inch) stick cinnamon, broken in bits
2 bay leaves, crushed
$1\frac{1}{2}$ cups sugar

Wash cucumbers and drain. Place in enamel kettle or heavy crock. Combine boiling water and salt; mix and pour over cucumbers. Let stand overnight. Drain cucumbers. Combine remaining ingredients in agate or enamel kettle; heat to boiling. Add cucumbers; let heat to boiling. Pack at once into hot, sterile glass jars. Fill jars with hot vinegar mixture; seal. Let stand 4 weeks or longer before using. Makes about 3 quarts.

NOTE: Old-time cooks added alum "the size of a pea" to each jar for crispness.

SWEET-SOUR SLICED CUCUMBER PICKLES

garnish baked oysters with these or serve with rarebit.

9 large cucumbers, washed, pared, sliced thin
4 large onions, washed, peeled, sliced thin
Salt
1 pint cider vinegar
1 cup (packed) brown sugar
1 teaspoon celery salt
1 teaspoon powdered ginger
2 teaspoons mustard seeds
1 teaspoon freshly-ground black pepper
1/2 teaspoon turmeric
1 teaspoon powdered cinnamon

Combine cucumbers and onions in agate or enamel kettle. Sprinkle with salt; cover and let stand 1 hour. Drain. Add remaining ingredients; mix. Heat slowly to boiling. Seal at once in hot sterile glass jars. Let stand a few weeks before using. Makes 4 pints.

WINE-VINEGAR PICKLES

this is a spicy-sweet pickle of unusual flavor.

2 quarts medium-sized (3- to 4-inch) cucumbers
Salt
12 peppercorns
3 tablespoons chopped fresh or dried tarragon
6 bay leaves
2 or 3 sprays fresh dill
10 whole cloves
2 sweet red or green peppers, washed, seeds removed, chopped
Wine vinegar

Wash cucumbers, drain, cover with fresh cold water, and let stand 6 to 8 hours. Drain; cover thickly with salt and let stand overnight. Next morning, shake and rub off salt. Pack closely in a 3-quart or 1-gallon stone jar or large glass jar, in layers, each layer sprinkled with the peppercorns, cloves, mixed herbs, and chopped peppers. Boil enough wine vinegar to cover them by 2 inches (about 2 quarts); pour hot over pickles. Cover and let stand 4 days. Drain off liquid, reheat to boiling, skim, and let cool. Pour over pickles again. Add more wine vinegar if necessary to cover pickles by 2 inches. Put a weight on the pickles; let stand in cool place at least 1 month. Can be longer. Makes 2 quarts pickles.

7

Pickled and Spiced Fruits

PICKLED AND SPICED FRUITS ARE SO WIDELY
popular today that any homemaker is tempted to try her
hand at producing a few jars for the winter menus. Many
of the long-established recipes were developed in this country from old English concoctions. The gardens, orchards,
plentiful spices, sugar, and cider vinegar of American farms
have always encouraged country housekeepers to vary the
old recipes, to create new ones, and to develop delicious
combinations which often took prizes at local state fairs.
Such recipes are included here for your sampling.

CANTALOUPE RIND PICKLE

a Colorado favorite, and just as good as watermelon pickle.

1 quart cantaloupe rind
Salt
1 cup water
1$\frac{1}{4}$ cups cider vinegar
2 cups sugar
1 (three-inch) stick cinnamon, broken
6 whole cloves
2 thin slices unpeeled orange, quartered, seeds removed
2 thin slices unpeeled lemon, quartered, seeds removed
1 tablespoon minced preserved ginger

Wash 1 large, or 2 small, cantaloupes; cut in quarters; cut out seeds and membrane. Remove all but half an inch of meat from rind. (Use the cut-out melon in fruit cup or salad.) Pare rind. Cut fruity rind in narrow strips, squares, or rounds. Cover with salted water, about 4 tablespoons salt to each quart cold water. Let soak overnight. Next morning drain well, rinse quickly under cold running water, drain, and measure.

Combine water, vinegar, sugar, and spices in an agate or enamel kettle. Boil until they form a thick sirup, about 20 minutes. Add orange, lemon, and ginger. Boil 1 minute. Add rind; let simmer about 5 minutes, then bring to boiling, and boil 1 minute. Spoon rind into hot sterile glass jars; spoon boiling sirup over the rind to fill the jars. Seal at once. Let stand a few weeks before serving. Makes about 1½ pints.

PENNSYLVANIA PICKLED PLUMS

to feature with curried lamb or chicken, or with shrimp salad.

3 pounds small greengage, blue, or red plums
1 pound sugar
1 (four-inch) stick cinnamon, broken
6 whole cloves
1 cup cider vinegar

Wash plums and drain. Prick each in several places with a large needle. Place plums in an agate or enamel kettle. Combine sugar, spices, and vinegar in another agate or enamel kettle; bring to boiling. Pour boiling hot over the plums. Let stand 15 minutes. Drain off liquid, bring to boiling, and pour again over plums. Let stand 15 minutes; drain off, reheat to boiling; add plums, let boil 5 minutes. Spoon into hot sterile glass jars; pour hot sirup over; seal at once. Let stand several weeks before using. Makes 2½ pints.

PICKLED PEACHES I

many savory uses as garnish or in fruit salads.

2 pounds (7 or 8) ripe peaches
Whole cloves
1 pound sugar
1 cup white or cider vinegar
1 cup water
2 (three-inch) sticks cinnamon

Scald peaches; pull skins off; leave whole and stick each with a clove. Combine sugar, vinegar, water, 6 cloves, and cinnamon in agate or enamel kettle. Boil 5 minutes, covered. Add peaches a few at a time; continue boiling gently until peaches are soft, about 15 to 20 minutes. Spoon peaches into hot sterile glass jars. Pour sirup over peaches to fill jars; seal at once. Let stand a few weeks before using. Makes 2 pints.

PICKLED APRICOTS

Use recipe opposite, but omit clove from each apricot. Watch timing, since apricots are more tender and need less cooking.

PICKLED PEACHES ·II

eat as dessert with pound cake or serve with roasts.

4 quarts (about 28) small ripe peaches
Boiling water
2 pounds sugar
1 pound light-brown sugar
3 cups cider vinegar
4 (three-inch) sticks cinnamon
2 tablespoons whole cloves

Wash peaches and drain. Place a few at a time in a sieve or strainer, lower into kettle of boiling water for about 1 minute; drain; rinse with cold water; remove skins. Boil sugars, vinegar, and cinnamon together in agate or enamel kettle 15 minutes. Place 4 or 5 peaches in sirup at one time until all are added and cook 5 minutes, or until tender. Spoon peaches into hot sterile glass jars; add few cloves to each jar; fill to overflowing with hot juice. Seal at once. Makes 4 quarts.

PICKLED SMALL SECKEL PEARS

serve as dessert, or as addition to salad and appetizer trays.

3½ pounds small seckel pears
2 cups sugar
2 cups (packed) brown sugar
I cup cider vinegar
I (two-inch) stick cinnamon
2 teaspoons whole cloves
I small piece ginger root
½ teaspoon powdered cinnamon
½ teaspoon powdered cloves
I blade mace

Wash pears; remove blossom end; leave stem on; do not peel. Cover with water; bring to boiling and boil 5 minutes. Drain, saving 1 cup of liquid. Add this to remaining ingredients in an agate or enamel kettle. Boil gently 5 minutes. Add pears; cook slowly, covered, until pears are tender and transparent, about 45 minutes. Pack into hot sterile glass jars; cover to over-flowing with hot sirup. Seal at once. Let stand a few weeks before using. Makes about 3 pints.

QUICK SPICED PEACHES

this needs no sealing. Just store in refrigerator for ready use.

I No. 2½ can cling peach halves
½ cup sugar
½ cup cider vinegar
I tablespoon mixed pickling spices

Drain peaches; save sirup. Add sugar, vinegar, and spices to sirup in agate or enamel kettle. Boil 10 minutes. Add drained peach halves; simmer gently 5 minutes. Remove from heat. Chill. Cover fruit and let stand in spiced sirup several hours or overnight, or longer. Makes about 2½ cups.

NOTE: Good with ice cream, as garnish with roasts, as part of fruit salad or fruit cup.

SPICED CRAB APPLES

a favorite with roast pork, ham, and game, and for the buffet table.

12 small crab apples with stems
1½ cups cider
½ cup wine vinegar or mild cider vinegar
1½ cups light-brown sugar
1 (three-inch) stick cinnamon
3 whole cloves
3 whole allspice
½ teaspoon powdered ginger
¼ teaspoon grated nutmeg
2 tablespoons lemon juice

Wash crab apples, drain, leave whole with stems on. Combine cider, vinegar, 1 cup sugar, and the spices in an agate or enamel saucepan; cover and boil gently 5 minutes. Add apples, cover again and cook gently until apples are soft but not broken, about 15 minutes. Remove apples to hot, sterile, glass jars as soon as tender. Add remaining half cup sugar and lemon juice to the sirup; boil 5 minutes or until sirup is slightly thickened. Pour over crab apples in jars to fill. Seal at once. Makes 2 pints.

SPICED FRESH CURRANTS

an old English favorite, fine with game, also with desserts.

4 quarts fresh ripe red or black currants
½ teaspoon whole cloves
1 (two-inch) stick cinnamon, broken
2 pounds sugar
1 pint cider vinegar

Wash and stem currants; tie spices in small cheesecloth bag; heat spices, sugar, and vinegar in agate or enamel kettle to boiling. Add currants; cook slowly, uncovered, until currants are bursting, about 20 minutes. Remove spice bag. Cook down a little to thicken, if necessary. Spoon into hot sterile glass jars. Makes about 6 pints.

NOTE: Try with cottage cheese, Philadelphia cream cheese, or the many variations of cream cheese which are imported, such as Swedish Hable. Superb together, on plain crackers or thin buttered toast.

SPICED GOOSEBERRIES

serve with clotted cream or as sweet on the sandwich tray.

2 quarts ripe gooseberries, washed and stemmed
1½ pounds (4⅛ cups packed) brown sugar
1 cup cider vinegar
½ teaspoon powdered cinnamon
½ teaspoon powdered cloves
½ teaspoon grated nutmeg

Pick over berries and drain. Combine sugar, vinegar, and spices in agate or enamel kettle; bring to boiling; add berries, a few at a time. Cook slowly until fruit is tender, about 40 minutes. Pour into hot sterile glass jars. Makes about 5 pints.

NOTE: Varieties of gooseberries differ in acidity. If you can find the large, pink-cheeked gooseberries, the above amount of sugar is just right. If the berries seem underripe and sour, add more sugar as needed. Taste the hot vinegar mixture before adding berries, to determine sweetness.

SPICED NECTARINES OR PEACHES

use in fruit cup and salad, as dessert, or as garnish for meat.

2 quarts firm ripe nectarines or small peaches
Whole cloves
2½ cups (packed) brown sugar
1 cup cider vinegar
1 (two-inch) stick cinnamon, broken

Wash fruit, peel nectarines. Scald peaches; peel. Stick a clove into each. Heat sugar, vinegar, cinnamon and 1 tablespoon cloves in agate or enamel kettle. When boiling add fruit. Cook until tender, about 10 minutes. Place in hot sterile glass jars. Pour hot sirup over to within half an inch of top. Seal at once. Let stand a few weeks before using. Makes about 3 pints.

SPICED PEAR CHIPS

more like a pear butter; delicious on hot toast or brioche.

2 pounds ripe Bartlett pears
2 cups sugar
2 tablespoons chopped preserved or candied ginger
I lemon, or
    I½ limes

Wash pears; remove stems and blossom ends; peel, quarter, core, and slice thin into glass or china bowl. Add sugar and ginger. Cover and let stand overnight. In the morning grate the peel of lemon or limes over the pears. Cut remaining white rind away from fruit, quarter, and remove seeds. Add fruit to pears. Mix and cook in enamel or agate kettle slowly, about 1½ hours, or until the consistency of marmalade. Stir frequently. Pour into small sterile glass jars or jelly glasses. Seal. Makes about 2 pints.

NOTE. Any ripe late-summer pear may be used in this recipe.

SPICED PEARS

use large or small seckel pears and serve as dessert.

2 cups white or cider vinegar
3 cups (packed) brown sugar
1½ teaspoons whole cloves
2 (three-inch) sticks cinnamon
4 pounds (about 15) pears, washed, peeled, cored, and quartered

Combine vinegar, sugar, and spices in an agate or enamel kettle. Heat to boiling, and let boil 5 minutes; add pears a few at a time; boil gently until pears are tender. Spoon pears into hot sterile glass jars; fill to running over with sirup. Seal at once. Makes 3 pints.

NOTE: There may be leftover juice or sirup. If so, save it to use in fruit salad dressings or sauces for cake.

SPICED PRUNES AND TOMATOES

one of the best for lunch-box sandwiches or as garnish for meat loaf.

3 cups drained cooked prunes
3 cups canned tomatoes with juice
2 cups granulated sugar
2 cups (packed) brown sugar
¼ teaspoon salt
1 teaspoon powdered cinnamon
½ teaspoon powdered cloves
3 tablespoons white or cider vinegar
1 cup coarsely-chopped walnuts

Cut prunes from pits into small pieces. Combine all ingredients, except walnuts, in an agate or enamel kettle. Cook slowly, uncovered, to desired consistency, about 45 minutes. Stir frequently with wooden or enamel spoon to prevent scorching. Add walnuts for last 5 minutes of cooking. Pour into sterile glass jars. Seal at once. Makes about 3 pints.

SPICED QUINCES

delicious, mild-sweet, for dessert or with hot biscuits.

5 pounds (about 10) quinces
3 pounds sugar
10 whole cloves
4 (three-inch) sticks cinnamon
Peel of 2 lemons, cut thin, finely-chopped

Wash quinces; core, peel, and slice thin. Cook covered, in agate or enamel kettle with water to cover half way, until fruit is almost tender, about 10 minutes. Drain sirup from quinces. Measure 2 cups of sirup, combine with sugar, spices, and lemon peel. Boil gently, covered, 5 minutes. Add the partly-cooked quinces and continue cooking slowly until fruit is soft, 10 to 15 minutes. Spoon into hot sterile glass jars; pour sirup over to fill. Seal at once. Makes 4 pints.

SUNDAY NIGHT STUFFED PEACHES

these are the "mangoes" of olden days, delicious, and novel.

6 medium-large ripe freestone peaches
3 tablespoons mustard seeds
3 tablespoons grated fresh or drained prepared horse-radish
2 cups sugar
1 cup (packed) brown sugar
1½ cups cider vinegar
1 cup water
2 lemons, unpeeled, sliced thin, seeds removed
1 (three-inch) stick cinnamon, broken
½ teaspoon powdered ginger
½ teaspoon powdered cloves
½ teaspoon powdered cinnamon

Scald peaches and pull off skins. Use small paring knife to work out peach stone; discard stones. Mix mustard seeds and horse-radish; fill peach centers; fasten openings with wooden picks. Combine remaining ingredients in agate or enamel kettle; boil until sirup is thickened, about 25 to 35 minutes. Place stuffed peaches in sterile wide-mouthed jar. Pour hot spiced vinegar over to cover; seal at once. Let stand a few weeks in cool dark place before using. Remove wooden picks before serving. Makes 1 quart.

NOTE: Whole canned peaches or apricots may be used in this recipe; use sirup from the can in place of water, and reduce sugar by half. Serve as a sweet-sour with buffet menu, or as garnish for roast.

WATERMELON PICKLE

one of the most popular of all old-time pickles.

7 cups (2 pounds) prepared watermelon rind
3 tablespoons salt
1 quart cold water
1 quart boiling water
1 pint white or cider vinegar
6 cups (3 pounds) sugar
1 teaspoon powdered cinnamon
1 teaspoon powdered cloves
2 tablespoons whole cloves
2 tablespoons whole allspice
5 (three-inch) sticks cinnamon, broken

Select a fine, ripe melon. Cut in eighths and cut out fruit. (Serve this in sections or for fruit cup.) Pare green and all the pink from rind. Cut rind in thin slices, then in strips or rounds. Measure 7 cups. Cover with 1 quart cold water to which the salt has been added. Cover and let stand overnight. Drain; cover with fresh water, cook 8 to 10 minutes; drain again. Combine the 1 quart boiling water, vinegar, sugar, powdered cinnamon, and powdered cloves in agate or enamel kettle. Tie whole spices in small cheesecloth bag and add to kettle. Bring to boiling and stir until sugar dissolves. Boil 5 minutes. Add drained rind. Boil gently until rind is transparent, about 45 minutes. Remove spice bag. Spoon fruit into hot sterile glass jars; seal at once. Let stand about 4 weeks before using. Makes about 2 pints.

8

Pickled and Spiced Vegetables

TERMS FOR PICKLED DISHES ARE USED LOOSELY.
Who can define a pickled fruit, a spiced vegetable when in
some cases both pickling fluids, that is, vinegars, and spices are
used? And of course, it doesn't matter. If you make a fine
spiced vegetable mixture and want to call it a pickle, there is
no reason why it should not be so called. Through long usage
and the family-to-family exchange of recipes through the
years terms have been carelessly applied, and recipes named
according to the ideas of the farm wife who prepared the
concoction and put it up in a stone jar.

EASY SPICED BEETS

don't make this unless you can use miniature cooked or canned beets.

3 cups cider vinegar

2 cups sugar

I cup light brown sugar

2 cups water

2 tablespoons mixed pickle spices

2 (one-inch) pieces stick cinnamon

2 tablespoons salt

3 quarts (about 12 pounds raw) very small cooked or canned beets

Mix all ingredients except beets in enamel or agate kettle. Bring to boiling, cover, boil 5 minutes. Add drained cooked or canned beets. Cover and boil quickly 8 to 10 minutes. Spoon beets into hot sterile glass jars; pour hot vinegar mixture over them. Seal at once. Let stand a month or longer before using. Makes about 3 quarts.

GINGERED TOMATO PRESERVES

as good at breakfast as at a moonlight barbecue supper.

2 quarts small yellow or red cherry tomatoes
Sugar
2 ounces green ginger root, scraped and cut in pieces
1½ lemons, unpeeled, sliced thin, seeds removed
2 cups water

Wash tomatoes and remove stems. Measure tomatoes; add 1½ cups of sugar for every quart of tomatoes. Combine ginger, lemons, and water; add to tomatoes and sugar; bring to boiling. Cover and cook slowly until tomatoes are transparent, about 1 hour. Uncover and let excess sirup cook down. Spoon into hot sterile glass jars; fill to overflowing; seal at once. Makes 2 pints.

NOTE: Mix any leftover sirup with cottage cheese for sandwiches.

SPICED GREEN BEANS

these add tang to salads or appetizer tray.

2 quarts green beans
Salt
3 cups white or cider vinegar
½ cup (packed) brown sugar
½ teaspoon salt
¼ teaspoon white pepper
½ teaspoon whole allspice
1 (two-inch) stick cinnamon, broken
½ tablespoon whole cloves

Wash beans. Remove any strings and tips. Leave beans whole. Cook in boiling salted water, 1 teaspoon salt to 1 quart water, until tender, 20 to 30 minutes. Drain and pack into hot sterile glass jars. Combine remaining ingredients in agate or enamel kettle; heat to boiling; pour over beans. Seal. Let stand several weeks before using. Makes about 4 pints.

NOTE: If you have beans in the garden, pick the immature tiny, slender beans and use in this recipe for a delicate, delicious pickle.

YELLOW TOMATO PRESERVES

recommended with hot roast beef, cold meats, cheese.

2 pounds smallest yellow egg-shaped tomatoes
1 ounce green ginger root
1/2 teaspoon powdered ginger
1 small lemon
2 1/2 cups sugar
3/4 cup (packed) brown sugar
1 1/2 cups water

Wash and drain tomatoes; do not scald and peel. Scrape ginger root and cut in small pieces. Wash lemon, slice thin, and remove seeds. Combine sugar and water in agate or enamel kettle; stir with wooden or enamel spoon over heat until sugar dissolves. Add ginger root, powdered ginger, and lemon. Bring to boiling; stir and boil 5 minutes. Add tomatoes. Cook until transparent. Spoon tomatoes into hot sterile jars. Skim sirup if necessary; pour over tomatoes to overflowing; seal at once. Let stand several weeks before using. Makes about 2 1/2 pints.

NOTE: You can use small cherry tomatoes in this recipe to make a sweet preserve, delectable with hot or cold meat, roast turkey, game. Fine as a spread with cottage cheese on gingerbread or crackers.

9

Relishes

A RELISH IS A COMPARATIVELY SIMPLE MIX-
ture of chopped vegetables; should be, by most recipes,
finely chopped. But with all mixtures in the general group
of pickling and spicing, the term "relish," is used loosely.
Generally, it means any spicy sour or sweet mixture served
as garnish or to spice up another food such as an aspic, cold
meats, sandwiches, or to add color and flavor to a serving
of meat. Its color is as important as its flavor in creating
appetite appeal—a spoonful of green pickle relish on a
sandwich plate, a spoonful of beet relish added to the cold
meat platter—these tell the hungry family that good flavor
is theirs, and contrast and variety, too.

COLD BEET RELISH

no cooking, but tang, color, good flavor in this relish.

4 cups finely-chopped or ground cooked or canned beets
4 cups finely-chopped or ground cabbage
½ cup prepared horse-radish
1 cup sugar
1 tablespoon salt
Cider vinegar

Combine beets and cabbage in bowl; add horse-radish, sugar, and salt. Toss and mix lightly. Pack into sterile glass jars. Pour vinegar in to cover, about ⅔ cup to each pint jar. Seal; let stand in dark cool place a few weeks before using. Makes 4 pints.

OHIO CORN RELISH

especially good with boiled beef or in sandwich mixtures.

1 large cucumber, washed, pared, and quartered
3 medium-sized onions, washed, peeled, and quartered
1 green pepper, washed, quartered, seeds and fiber removed
3 cups sweet corn, freshly cut from cob
2 medium-sized tomatoes, scalded and peeled
1 cup sugar
2 tablespoons salt
$\frac{1}{2}$ teaspoon black pepper
1 cup cider vinegar
$\frac{1}{2}$ cup water
$\frac{1}{2}$ teaspoon turmeric
$\frac{1}{2}$ tablespoon mustard seeds

Put cucumber, onions, and green pepper through grinder together, using medium knife. Combine with corn and tomatoes in agate or enamel kettle. Add remaining ingredients, mix, and bring to boiling. Stir almost constantly with wooden or enamel spoon until sugar dissolves. Then cook slowly, covered, over medium heat, about 45 minutes. Corn should be cooked tender. Pour into hot sterile glass jars and seal at once. Let stand at least 4 weeks before using. Makes about 2½ pints.

NOTE: Use very fresh, tender young sweetcorn for best results. Cut corn from cobs, but do not scrape. If canned corn is used, drain well. If quick-frozen corn is used, thaw and drain before mixing.

OHIO MINT RELISH

a classic accompaniment for hot or cold lamb.

2 cups cider vinegar
2 cups sugar
½ tablespoon dry mustard
2 large ripe sweet apples, washed, cored, and finely diced
1 medium-sized very ripe tomato, scalded, peeled, and chopped
½ cup finely-diced washed and peeled onion
½ cup seedless raisins, soaked and drained
¼ teaspoon salt
1 cup chopped, washed fresh mint leaves

Scald vinegar in an agate or enamel kettle; add sugar and mustard. Stir and remove from heat. Let cool slightly. Pour over remaining ingredients, mix, spoon into hot sterile glass jars, and seal at once. Makes 2 pints.

PICKAWAY COUNTY PEPPER RELISH

a prize-winner at the State Fair in Columbus, Ohio.

12 large green peppers
6 sweet red peppers
Boiling water
5 large sweet Spanish onions, washed, peeled, and chopped fine
2½ cups sugar
2 cups cider vinegar
1½ tablespoons salt

Wash peppers; cut in strips; remove seeds and membrane. Put peppers through food grinder using medium blade. Cover with boiling water; let stand 5 minutes; drain well, pressing water out. Cover with boiling water again; let stand 15 minutes; drain thoroughly. Combine pepper with chopped onions. Mix sugar, vinegar, and salt in agate or enamel kettle; heat to boiling. Add peppers and onions. Stir; bring to boiling; boil, uncovered, 20 minutes. Spoon into hot sterile glass jars and seal at once. Makes 6 pints.

QUICK CHRISTMAS RELISH

can be used as soon as made or kept handy in refrigerator.

6 medium-sized green peppers
6 medium-sized sweet red peppers
2 stalks celery
2 medium-sized Bermuda onions
¾ tablespoon salt
¾ cup sugar
1½ cups cider vinegar
½ teaspoon freshly-ground black pepper
½ teaspoon celery salt

Wash vegetables and drain. Cut peppers in half; remove seeds and fiber. Cut leaves from celery. Peel onions. Put all vegetables through food grinder, using medium knife. Combine remaining ingredients in an agate or enamel kettle; heat to boiling; add ground vegetables. Boil 10 minutes (loosely covered). Stir frequently with wooden or enamel spoon. Seal at once in hot sterile glass jars. Makes 4 pints.

RAISIN-RHUBARB RELISH

to feature at buffet and barbecue suppers.

1 cup (packed) brown sugar
1 cup cider vinegar
1 cup water
1/2 teaspoon allspice
1/2 teaspoon whole cloves
1 (four-inch) stick cinnamon, broken
1/2 teaspoon mustard seeds
1/4 teaspoon celery seeds
1 cup chopped peeled onions
1 1/2 cups sliced fresh or thawed quick-frozen rhubarb
1 cup seedless raisins

Combine sugar, vinegar, water, and spices and seeds in an agate or enamel kettle, and boil about 2 minutes. Add onions and rhubarb; cover and cook slowly 30 minutes or longer. Rinse and drain raisins; add to hot mixture; cook 10 minutes uncovered. Stir a few times with wooden or enamel spoon. Serve when cold. Or seal while hot in hot sterile glasses. Makes about 2 pints.

NOTE: If quick-frozen rhubarb is used, thaw and drain well before adding as directed.

UNCOOKED TOMATO RELISH

a hot and savory flavor to add to salad, or as garnish to an aspic.

6 ripe tomatoes, washed, cored, and quartered
1 green pepper, washed, seeds and fiber discarded
1 small hot pepper, chopped
4 medium-sized stalks celery, leaves removed
3 medium-sized hot-type onions, washed, peeled, and quartered
1/2 cup finely-cut washed fresh parsley
1 tablespoon salt
1/4 cup sugar
2 cups white or cider vinegar

Put all vegetables through food grinder, using medium knife. Mix with parsley, salt, sugar, and vinegar in an agate or enamel kettle, or a large bowl. Do not cook. Pour into sterile glass jars; cover or seal. Let stand in a cool place for a few weeks before using. Makes about 3 pints.

10

Quick Relishes

From Pantry and Refrigerator Staples

IF YOUR STORE OF SUMMER-MADE CANNED REL-
ishes is used up, you can still delight the family and guests
with crisp, good flavor with these "quickies" made from
kitchen staples. With prepared horse-radish, mustard, and
other good condiments and such on-hand pantry items as
pickles, olives, and celery, quick-relishes are easily concocted.
About thirty such are offered here to busy cooks who may
not have time, when garden vegetables are at their best, to
put up enough for the winter's meals. Quick-made relishes
can be a hostess's best friend.

APPLE, ORANGE, AND MINT RELISH

fresh, fruity flavor to spice a platter of cold meats.

1 orange
1 cup applesauce
½ cup chopped washed fresh mint leaves

Grate orange, chop pulp, and remove seeds. Combine peel and pulp with applesauce; add mint. Makes about 2 cups.

APPLESAUCE AND RAISIN RELISH

garnish for open-face sandwiches of duck, turkey, cream cheese.

1 cup applesauce
½ cup seedless raisins, soaked and drained
2 tablespoons grated orange peel
½ teaspoon crushed dried marjoram

Combine all ingredients. Makes about 1½ cups.

CALIFORNIA CRANBERRY RELISH

keep handy in refrigerator for sandwich tray.

1 pound cranberries
1 cup seedless raisins
1 lemon
1 cup sugar
1/8 teaspoon salt

Rinse cranberries, raisins, and lemon. Cut lemon into lengthwise wedges and remove seeds. Put fruits through grinder, using medium knife. Blend in sugar and salt. Let stand in bowl or glass jar, covered, 1 hour or longer before serving. Makes about 1 quart.

CANDIED ORANGE PEEL RELISH

serve with hot or cold roast duck.

1/2 cup finely-cut candied orange peel
1/4 cup prepared horse-radish
1/2 cup applesauce

Combine all ingredients. Makes about 1 1/4 cups.

CANNED PLUM RELISH

serve cold with any roast.

2 or 3 canned greengage plums, drained
I or 2 small sweet pickles
Curry-seasoned French dressing

Cut plums from pits; chop pickles. Combine plums and pickles; moisten with the French dressing. Makes about 1½ cups.

NOTE: Vary by adding finely-chopped almonds and orange peel to plum mixture.

CARROT AND PARSLEY RELISH

for hot broiled fish or lamb chops.

I cup grated scraped carrots
2 tablespoons finely-cut fresh parsley
I tablespoon finely-cut chives
I tablespoon finely-cut pickled onions
½ teaspoon Worcestershire sauce
French dressing
Thick sour cream

Combine carrots, parsley, chives, and onions. Add Worcestershire to French dressing and moisten carrot mixture. Add just enough very thick sour cream to hold mixture together. Serve very cold. Makes about 1¼ cups.

CATSUP AND ONION RELISH

for hot barbecued meats and baked spareribs.

1 cup tomato catsup
1/2 cup finely-grated washed and peeled onion
1/4 cup finely-chopped washed green pepper, seeds and fiber
   discarded
1/4 cup finely-chopped stuffed olives
1/2 teaspoon dried oregano

Combine and mix all ingredients. Makes about 2 cups.

CAULIFLOWER AND MIXED
PICKLE RELISH

so good with hot roast veal and cold veal sandwiches.

1 cup finely-chopped raw cauliflower
1/2 cup drained mixed pickle or India relish
1/4 cup finely-chopped stuffed olives
Mayonnaise

Combine cauliflower, pickle or relish, and olives. Blend
with mayonnaise. Makes about 1 3/4 cups.

CELERY AND PEPPER RELISH

delicious with baked or scalloped oysters, or meat pie.

6 stalks celery, washed and chopped
2 green peppers, washed, chopped, seeds and fiber discarded
1 canned pimiento, drained and chopped fine
2 tablespoons prepared horse-radish
1 cup tiny pickled onions
1/2 teaspoon oregano
Durkee's Mustard Dressing

The success of this relish depends on very fine chopping of celery and peppers. Combine all ingredients; add the special dressing or your favorite mustard sauce to moisten and blend. Makes 3½ to 4 cups.

CHERRY PRESERVE RELISH

to serve with roast duck, pork, or hot sausages.

1 cup dark cherry preserves
1/4 cup sliced blanched almonds
1/4 cup grated orange peel
2 tablespoons finely-cut washed mint leaves
Orange juice

Combine preserves, almonds, orange peel, and mint leaves. Thin, if necessary, with orange juice. Makes about 1½ cups.

CHILI SAUCE RELISH

serve on barbecued meats, and with sandwiches.

1 cup chili sauce
2 tablespoons prepared horse-radish
1/4 cup finely-chopped sweet pickles
1/2 teaspoon Worcestershire sauce
1/4 cup chopped cucumber
1/4 cup chopped pickled onions

Combine all ingredients and mix well. Makes about 1¾ cups.

CHIVES AND CABBAGE RELISH

especially good with cold ham, or cold meat pie.

1/2 cup finely-cut or chopped chives
2 cups finely-chopped crisp cabbage
1/2 cup thinly-sliced stuffed olives
1 tablespoon poppy seeds
Russian dressing

Combine chives, cabbage, olives, and poppy seeds. Moisten with Russian dressing. Makes about 3 cups.

CRANBERRY AND ORANGE JUICE RELISH

to serve very cold with any hot roast.

1 quart cranberries
½ cup powdered sugar
2 cups orange juice

Wash berries, drain, and chop or grind fine. Turn into bowl; sprinkle with sugar; cover with orange juice. Cover and chill in refrigerator 2 or more hours. Stir once or twice during that time. Drain. (Use juice in mixing other relishes or thinning cream cheese for a sandwich spread.) Makes about 1 quart.

CRANBERRY RELISH

a winter favorite with roasts

1 quart cranberries
1 large orange
4 ripe eating apples
3 cups sugar

Wash cranberries and drain. Wash orange, slice, and remove seeds. Wash, pare, and core apples. Put all together through a grinder, using medium knife. Mix with sugar. Store in glass jar or bowl in refrigerator. Will keep a week or longer. Makes about 2 quarts.

CUCUMBER AND ONION RELISH

serve with baked oysters, meat loaf, curried dishes.

1 large cucumber, washed, pared, chopped very fine
1 large onion, washed, peeled, and chopped
1 tablespoon finely-cut parsley
1 tablespoon finely-cut chives
Tart French dressing, or oil and vinegar

Combine vegetables and herbs. Moisten with French dressing, or equal parts of oil and vinegar. Makes 1 cup.

CURRANT AND ORANGE PEEL RELISH

serve with cold boiled beef tongue, or hot barbecued meats.

1 cup dried currants, washed, soaked, drained
1 cup grated orange peel
1 or 2 small sweet gherkins, cut very fine
French dressing

Combine currants, orange peel, and pickles. Moisten with French dressing. Makes about 2½ cups.

FRESH CURRANT AND MINT RELISH

for game, lamb, veal, or chicken.

1 cup washed fresh currants, picked from stems, slightly crushed
½ cup finely-cut mint leaves
Powdered sugar
French dressing or orange juice
Thick sour cream

Combine currants and mint in bowl; sprinkle with sugar; let stand covered in refrigerator 2 to 3 hours. Moisten with a very little French dressing or orange juice. Serve with thick sour cream. Makes about 1½ cups.

DILL PICKLE, CAPERS, BEET RELISH

for cold boiled salmon, tuna fish mold, or boiled beef.

2 dill pickles (three-inch or little larger) chopped fine
1 tablespoon capers, chopped
1 tablespoon beet horse-radish, or
    ½ tablespoon prepared horse-radish, and
    1 tablespoon chopped pickled beets
1 cup French dressing

Combine pickles, capers, beet horse-radish or horse-radish and beets. Stir into French dressing. Makes about 1¼ cups.

GHERKINS AND STUFFED OLIVES RELISH

nice with tomato aspic, other aspics, or cold cuts.

6 to 8 small sweet pickles, chopped very fine
1 cup chopped stuffed olives
6 to 8 small pickled onions, chopped fine
Durkee's Mustard Dressing

Combine pickles, olives, and onions. Add enough dressing to bind. Makes about 2 cups.

GINGER AND PICKLE RELISH

delicious with curries.

½ cup finely-chopped preserved ginger
1 or 2 small sweet pickles, chopped fine
½ cup grated orange peel
French dressing

Combine ginger, pickles, and orange peel. Moisten to taste with French dressing. Makes about 1¼ cups.

GREEN PEPPER AND GRAPEFRUIT RELISH

a garnish for salmon mousse, or hot sea-food canapés.

1 large green pepper, washed, seeds and fiber removed
1 cup chopped drained grapefruit sections, seeds removed
1/4 cup finely-cut ripe olives
1/4 cup finely-cut sweet gherkins

Chop pepper as fine as possible; combine with remaining ingredients. Makes about 2 cups.

MINT CHERRY RELISH

try this in place of mint jelly with broiled chops.

1/2 cup finely-chopped green mint cherries
1/4 cup finely-chopped peeled orange, seeds removed
1/4 cup applesauce

To be appetizing, these minted cherries should be cut or chopped into very fine bits. Combine all ingredients. Makes about 1 cup.

MUSHROOM AND RADISH RELISH

to serve as a canapé spread.

1 cup thinly-sliced and diced canned mushrooms
1/2 cup diced radishes
2 tablespoons diced pared cucumber
1 tablespoon cut chives
Russian dressing

Combine mushrooms, radishes, cucumber, and chives. Moisten with Russian dressing. Makes about 1¾ cups.

MUSHROOM RELISH

serve with cold roast turkey, or as canapé spread.

1 cup thinly-sliced and chopped canned mushrooms
1/2 cup diced ripe olives
1/4 cup diced sweet pickles
1 tablespoon minced canned pimiento
Mayonnaise

Combine mushrooms, olives, pickles, and pimiento. Add enough mayonnaise to moisten and hold together. Makes about 2 cups.

OLIVE AND HORSE-RADISH RELISH

especially good with fish.

1 cup chopped ripe olives
1 tablespoon prepared horse-radish
½ canned pimiento, minced fine
Mayonnaise

Blend olives, horse-radish, and pimiento. Add just enough mayonnaise to bind. Makes about 1¼ cups.

ORANGE AND ONION RELISH

use for turkey and chicken sandwiches.

1 seedless orange, peeled and chopped fine
1 Bermuda onion, peeled and chopped fine
1 teaspoon finely-cut chives
French dressing made with orange or lemon juice

Combine orange, onion, and chives. Moisten with French dressing. Makes about 1 cup.

PARSLEY AND ALMOND RELISH

for hot broiled salmon steaks.

1 cup finely-cut washed fresh parsley
¼ cup sliced almonds
French dressing
Mayonnaise

Combine parsley and almonds; moisten with highly-seasoned French dressing; mix to coat well. Then combine with a little mayonnaise. Chill. Serve very cold. Makes about 1¼ cups.

PEPPER, PICKLE, AND CABBAGE RELISH

serve with hot meat loaf, meat pie, or boiled tongue.

1 sweet red pepper
1 green pepper
1 cup finely-chopped crisp cabbage
1 small cucumber, chopped fine
1 or 2 gherkins, chopped fine
French dressing

Wash peppers, drain, cut open, and remove seeds and fiber. Chop or cut peppers into very fine bits. Combine with cabbage, cucumber, and gherkins. Moisten with French dressing. Have all ingredients cold. Makes about 2¼ cups.

QUICK MINTED RAISIN RELISH

serve with hot or cold lamb.

1 cup seedless raisins
Large handful washed fresh mint leaves
2 tablespoons India relish

Rinse raisins and mint; drain thoroughly. Put through food grinder, using medium knife. Mix with India relish. Keep in refrigerator. Makes about 1 cup.

QUICK MUSTARD PICKLE

add this to the salad tray.

4 gherkins, cut in half-inch slices
½ cup tiny pickled onions
¼ cup chopped cooked green beans, or
    Few cooked cauliflowerets
Durkee's Mustard Dressing

Combine vegetables; moisten and mix with enough dressing to bind. Makes about 1¼ cups.

SPANISH PICKLE RELISH

delicious with hot broiled fish.

1 or 2 Spanish onions, washed, peeled, chopped fine
1 sweet red pepper, washed, chopped, seeds and fiber removed
6 to 8 olives, chopped
1/2 teaspoon oregano

Combine onions, pepper, olives, and oregano. Blend with enough highly-seasoned French dressing to make about 1 cup. Serve very cold. Makes about 1 cup.

SWEET MELON RELISH

use as relish on fruit salad platter.

1 cup diced cantaloupe or honeydew melon
1/4 cup finely-cut mint leaves
1/4 cup finely-diced candied or preserved ginger
French dressing made with orange juice

Combine melon, mint leaves, and ginger. Moisten with French dressing. Makes 1 1/2 cups.

Sauces

THESE SPICY SAUCES HAVE MANY USES IN MENU making. Chili sauce belongs with a savory hamburger, with spareribs, with barbecued meats. It makes a welcome addition to the sandwich maker's tray, either added as a dressing to the sandwich itself, or blended with mild fillings such as cheese, chopped raw or cooked vegetables, and chopped leftover chicken, fish, or meat. A spoonful added to a mild white sauce can change it to a tangy sauce for fish, meat, and chicken or lamb croquettes. And add a little of any of these sauces to your favorite French dressing, stir to mix, use on a raw vegetable salad.

CHILI SAUCE

dark and more like chutney than commercial red chili sauce.

12 ripe tomatoes, scalded and peeled
3 large onions, peeled
2 green peppers, cut in half, seeds and fiber removed
1 pint cider vinegar
1 cup sugar
1 tablespoon salt
1½ teaspoons each powdered ginger, cloves, allspice

Chop vegetables fine, or put through grinder using fine knife. Combine with vinegar, sugar, and salt in agate or enamel kettle. Cook slowly, about 1¾ hours, or until thick. Stir and skim frequently with wooden or enamel spoon. About 15 minutes before removing from heat, stir in spices. Seal in hot sterile glass jars. Makes 4 pints.

MONTANA CENTURY SAUCE

with tang, like chutney or old-time chili sauce.

6 large ripe tomatoes, scalded and skinned
6 large eating apples, washed, peeled, cored, quartered
6 medium-sized onions washed and peeled
4 green peppers washed, quartered, seeds and fiber removed
4 sweet red peppers washed, quartered, seeds and fiber removed
1 cup seedless raisins
1 pint cider vinegar
1 cup sugar
2 tablespoons salt
1 teaspoon powdered cinnamon
½ teaspoon powdered cloves
½ teaspoon ground nutmeg
½ teaspoon powdered ginger

Put tomatoes, apples, onions, peppers, and raisins through food grinder, using medium knife, or chop very fine. Heat remaining ingredients in agate or enamel kettle. Add vegetables; cook uncovered, slowly, about 1 hour. Stir frequently with wooden or enamel spoon. Seal in hot sterile glass jars. Makes 5 pints.

PEACH AND TOMATO CHILI SAUCE

a new flavor. Can be made any time. Delicious with meats.

1 No. 2½ can cling peach slices
4 cups chopped peeled ripe, or canned, tomatoes
1 cup diced washed and peeled onions
1 cup white or cider vinegar
1 teaspoon salt
1 cup sugar
2 tablespoons mixed pickling spices

Drain peaches and chop. Combine sirup, peaches, tomatoes, onions, vinegar, salt, and sugar in agate or enamel kettle. Tie spices in small cheesecloth bag; add to kettle. Bring to boiling, cover, and simmer 2 hours, stirring occasionally with wooden or enamel spoon. Remove spice bag; continue cooking, uncovered, to reduce liquid and reach desired thickness. Seal hot in sterile glass jars. Makes 2½ pints.

Vinegars

VINEGAR IS AN ACID LIQUID USED IN SEASON-
ing and pickling. Its flavor and acidity vary according to
the kind of fermented juice from which it is made. Of the
commercial types, cider vinegar—soured apple cider—has
long been the favorite; distilled white or very light vinegar,
preferred by some cooks, is milder than cider vinegar. The
hearty malt vinegar, made from malt, barley, or other ce-
real, golden brown like apple cider vinegar, is also excellent. Wine vinegars, herb and fruit vinegars, such as pear,
grape, or cherry, are more popular for salad dressings and
certain sauces than for general cookery.

Because by any name vinegars differ in strength and flavor, it is well to experiment a little when using them, to make sure the tartness and flavor are what you want. You can flavor white, wine, and cider vinegar with herbs, spices, and vegetables. For instance, for celery vinegar add finely-chopped celery leaves to cider vinegar. Boil gently five minutes in an enamel kettle; let stand about three weeks in a covered jar, in the kitchen. Strain and bottle. Fresh mint leaves, fresh nasturtium seeds, or herbs may be combined with cider vinegar, or with wine to make other good mixtures.

In making all seed vinegars—caraway, cardamom, mustard, or celery—crush seeds in a mortar, or in the wide-mouthed glass jar in which you are making the vinegar. Use wooden spoon to crush seeds.

CARAWAY VINEGAR

vary salad dressings with this vinegar.

3 tablespoons caraway seeds
1 quart white wine vinegar

Mash seeds in a large glass jar. Heat wine almost to boiling. Pour over seeds, stirring and mashing with wooden spoon. Leave about a 2-inch space at the top of the jar. Cover tightly. Let stand in warm kitchen 10 days. Shake jar once each day. Taste at end of 10 days. If not flavorful enough, strain out seeds and replace with fresh crushed seeds. Cover again; let stand a few more days. Strain through fine sieve or wet doubled cheesecloth, or filter paper. Pour into sterile bottles, cork, and keep in cool place. Makes 1 quart.

NOTE: In making other seed vinegars—mustard, celery, or cardamom—follow the same proportions as for caraway vinegar.

COUNTRY BASIL VINEGAR

if you can get fresh basil, no reason this can't be made in town.

Handful fresh basil leaves
1 quart wine, or
    1 quart wine vinegar

Wash and drain leaves. Fill a glass jar almost full. Bruise the leaves in the jar by mashing and stirring with a wooden spoon. Heat wine or vinegar almost to boiling. Pour over leaves to cover, but keep about a 2-inch space at the top. Cover tightly. Let stand in warm kitchen 10 days. Shake jar once each day. Taste at end of 10 days. If not flavorful enough, strain out herb and replace with fresh leaves, crushed and bruised. Cover again; let stand a few more days. Strain through sieve, then through wet doubled cheesecloth or filter paper. Pour into sterile bottles, cork, and keep in cool place. Makes 1 quart.

GARLIC VINEGAR

an easy way to add garlic to the salad bowl.

4 garlic buds
1 teaspoon salt
1 tablespoon powdered cloves
1 teaspoon freshly-ground black pepper
1 teaspoon caraway seeds, crushed
1 quart wine or wine vinegar

Wash garlic, peel, crush in 1½-quart glass jar which has tight-fitting cover. Add salt, cloves, and pepper, and mix. Add crushed seeds; mix well. Heat wine or wine vinegar almost to boiling and pour over mixture. Cover; let stand 1 week in cool place. Strain. Pour into sterile bottles. Cork well. Makes about 1 quart.

MINT VINEGAR

heat and serve with hot or cold roast lamb or use in salad dressings.

1 quart cider vinegar
1 cup sugar
2 cups washed fresh mint or spearmint leaves

Heat vinegar and sugar together in agate or enamel kettle; crush leaves and add. Stir with enamel spoon, crushing mint against bottom of kettle. Boil about 5 minutes. Strain and pour into sterile bottles. Cork well. Makes about 1 quart.

TARRAGON VINEGAR

gives unusual flavor to salad dressings and sauces.

2 cups fresh tarragon leaves
1 pint wine vinegar
2 cloves
½ small garlic clove

Wash tarragon, drain, break or crush slightly in a bowl. Add vinegar, cloves, and garlic. Cover; let stand 24 hours. Remove garlic. Cover; let stand in cool dark place 2 weeks. Strain through cheesecloth or filter paper. Pour into sterile bottles. Cork tightly. Makes about 1 pint.

NOTE: To use dried tarragon, moisten leaves with a little hot water in a bowl; crush and mix as directed. Dried leaves make a good tarragon vinegar, but not so pungent and lively as fresh leaves.

OTHER HERB VINEGARS: Mint, or a mixture of your favorite herbs, may be used in place of tarragon in this recipe. Good combinations are burnet, basil, marjoram, dill, and caraway seeds—any two. Omit garlic from all these, and remove cloves after 24 hours.

RECOMMENDED COMBINATIONS: 1 part fresh tarragon, 2 parts lemon balm. One part tarragon, 2 parts each basil, chopped chives, and burnet. Equal parts thyme, chopped chives, and basil. For a cucumber-flavored vinegar (so good in salad dressings) use burnet leaves or seeds. Add this vinegar to fish sauces in place of lemon juice when called for in a recipe.

TO MAKE YOUR OWN WINE VINEGARS

For red wine vinegar, buy 1 quart claret. For white wine vinegar, buy 1 quart sauterne. If you have the "mother" from your last bottle of store vinegar, add that to the wine bottle. Cover the opening of the bottle with cheesecloth. Set the bottle away in a dark warmish place, such as kitchen cupboard. Let stand all winter, or all summer; at least 4 months. Good flavored vinegar results. Without the "mother" from the bought vinegar, let your wine stand at least 5 months—longer if necessary. Taste to decide whether it is sour enough.

Index

Index